MARQUETTE, JACQUES
jB
MAR

Donaldson-Forbes, Jeff
Jacques Marquett and Louis
Jolliet

Famous Explorers™

Jacques Marquette and Louis Jolliet

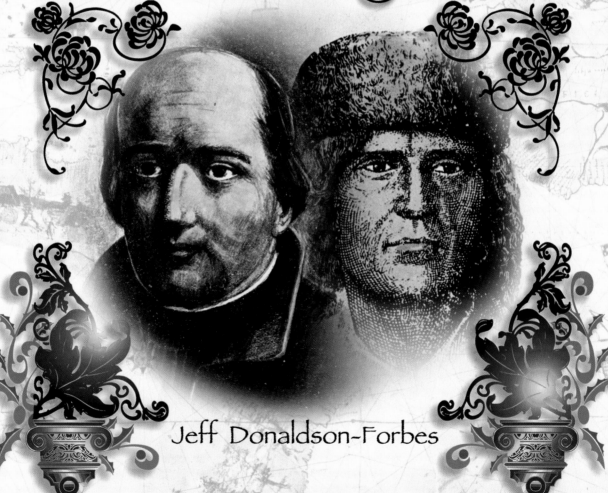

Jeff Donaldson-Forbes

The Rosen Publishing Group's
PowerKids Press™
New York

To Orlando Grant Whitcomb-Worden

Published in 2002 by The Rosen Publishing Group, Inc.
29 East 21st Street, New York, NY 10010

First Edition

Book Design: Maria E. Melendez and Felicity Erwin
Project Editors: Kathy Campbell, Jennifer Landau, Jason Moring, Jennifer Quasha

Photo Credits: Cover and title page, pp. 7 (bottom), 8 (left), 9 (top), 11, 12 (top), 15 (bottom), 19 (top), 19 (bottom), 20 (top) © North Wind Picture Archives; pp. 5 (top), 7, (top), 10, 13, 16 (top), 17 © Bettmann/CORBIS; p. 4 (bottom) © Baldwin H. Ward & Kathryn C. Ward/CORBIS; p. 12 (bottom) © SuperStock; pp. 15 (top), 16 (bottom), 20 (bottom) © N. Carter/North Wind Picture Archives; p. 15 (map) by Maria E. Melendez; p. 18 © CORBIS/Bettmann.

Donaldson-Forbes, Jeff.
Jacques Marquette and Louis Jolliet / Jeff Donaldson-Forbes.— 1st ed.
  p. cm. — (Famous explorers)
Includes index.
Summary: A brief biography of the seventeenth–century French explorers who were the first Europeans to locate and chart the Mississippi River.
  ISBN 0–8239–5835–3   2426202
1. Marquette, Jacques, 1637–1675—Juvenile literature. 2. Jolliet, Louis, 1645–1700—Juvenile literature. 3. Canada—Discovery and exploration—Juvenile literature. 4. Mississippi River Valley—Discovery and exploration—Juvenile literature. 5. Canada—History—To 1763 (New France)—Juvenile literature. 6. Mississippi River Valley—History—To 1803—Juvenile literature. 7. Explorers—America—Biography—Juvenile literature. 8. Explorers—France—Biography—Juvenile literature. [1. Marquette, Jacques, 1637–1675. 2. Jolliet, Louis, 1645–1700. 3. Mississippi River—Discovery and exploration. 4. Explorers.] I. Title. II. Series.
  F1030.2 .D59 2002
  977'.01'0922—dc21
                                                                00–012441

Contents

1   Young Marquette   5

2   A Mission in New France   6

3   Young Jolliet   9

4   Choosing an Explorer's Life   10

5   Stories of the Mississippi   13

6   The Journey Begins   14

7   Smoking in Peace   17

8   Into the Mississippi   18

9   Dangerous Water   21

10   Returning Home   22

    Glossary   23

    Index   24

    Web Sites   24

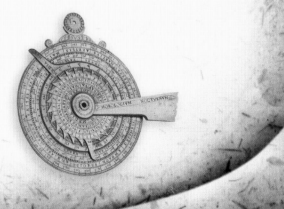

Young Marquette

Jacques Marquette was born in 1637, in the town of Laon, France. His father was a lawyer who provided a good life for his large family. Marquette had two older sisters and three younger brothers. At nine years old, Marquette began attending a **Jesuit** school in the town of Reims, France. The Jesuit priests were well-known **missionaries** and teachers. Marquette was an excellent student who studied math and **geography**. He also learned languages, including Latin and Greek. In October 1654, when Marquette was 17 years old, he moved to the town of Nancy, France. In Nancy, Marquette studied at a Jesuit college to become a priest. Finally he taught at the Jesuit school in Reims. Although Marquette was successful as a teacher, he dreamed of becoming a missionary.

Above: *This is a painting of Jacques Marquette as a young man.*
Left: *This painting shows Marquette's home as it looked in 1673.*

A Mission in New France

During their **expeditions** to New France, today called Canada, French explorers met native people who were not Christians. In the 1600s, the priests wanted to **convert** these people to Christianity. They did this by building **missions** in New France and converting Native Americans to Christianity. In March 1666, 29-year-old Marquette was **ordained** as a priest and was given the title Father. In August 1666, he sailed from the French town of La Rochelle. In northern Quebec, at Three Rivers, he studied the language of Native Americans who lived in the region. In 1668, Father Marquette traveled west and founded the mission of Sault Sainte Marie near Lake Huron and Lake Superior. In 1671, he founded another mission, named Saint Ignace, between Lake Huron and Lake Michigan.

These two pictures show Jesuit missionaries preaching to Native Americans. The man preaching in the top picture is Father Marquette.

Young Jolliet

Louis Jolliet was born in 1645, in a French **settlement** near Quebec. When Jolliet was six years old, his father died. Jolliet's mother married a successful **merchant**. Jolliet's stepfather owned land on Ile d'Orleans, an island in the Saint Lawrence River in Quebec. Ile d'Orleans was home to many Native Americans. Jolliet spent time on Ile d'Orleans, so it is likely that he began speaking Native American languages at a young age. During Jolliet's childhood, Quebec was the center of business for the French fur trade. The French traded goods with Native Americans, who supplied the French with animal furs. The furs were sent back to Europe where they were sold and used to make clothing. Native Americans were part of the day-to-day life in Quebec, and Jolliet grew up knowing a lot about them.

 Above: *This is a portrait of Louis Jolliet.* Left: *This is a photograph of Louis Jolliet's home as it looks today.*

Choosing an Explorer's Life

Like Marquette, Jolliet was a good student who attended a Jesuit school. He studied writing, mathematics, and Latin. Jolliet was a talented musician who played the **harpsichord**, the flute, and the trumpet. He enjoyed drawing and making maps. When he was 17 years old, Jolliet began studying to become a Jesuit priest. He also had dreams of exploring the western regions of New France. Finally his desire to explore was greater than his desire to become a priest. Jolliet asked to be released from his studies, and his Jesuit teachers agreed. In 1668, Jolliet set out to join his brothers, Adrien and Zacharie, who were successful fur traders at Three Rivers. The leaders in New France noticed the

Above: *Jean Baptiste Talon, shown in this picture, asked Louis Jolliet's brother to look for copper near Lake Superior.* Right: *This map of the Great Lakes was made by the Jesuits.*

success of the Jolliet brothers. In 1669, the French **lieutenant governor**, Jean Baptiste Talon, asked Jolliet's brother Adrien to search for copper near Lake Superior. Adrien did not find any copper, and while sailing home, he vanished. Sadly, he was never heard from again. After his brother's disappearance, Jolliet traveled west and continued fur trading near the mission at Sault Sainte Marie.

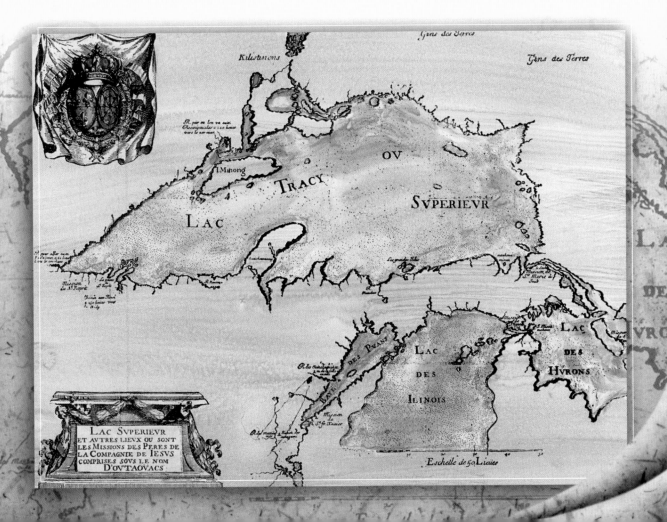

Stories of the Mississippi

European explorers in the seventeenth century believed that there might be a water route through North America that led to China. They hoped that the water route would allow Europe to trade with China for silk and spices. In New France, the Native Americans told stories of a great river called the Mississippi. The French thought that the Mississippi might be the water route to China. In 1672, Jean Baptiste Talon, the French lieutenant governor, chose Jolliet to lead an expedition to search for the Mississippi River. Talon told Jolliet to go to the mission at Saint Ignace. A priest from Saint Ignace would join the expedition as a missionary. The priest was Father Jacques Marquette.

 Above: *This is a statue of Louis Jolliet.* Top Left: *This picture shows Chinese women in the silk-making trade.* Bottom Left: *This is a map of ship routes for the seventeenth-century spice trade.*

The Journey Begins

On December 8, 1672, Jolliet arrived at the mission at Saint Ignace. He met with Father Marquette and they planned an expedition that would leave in the spring. Jolliet returned to his home in Sault Sainte Marie that winter. He waited until the weather was warm enough to break the ice that froze the lakes and rivers. Jolliet and his men then sailed to Saint Ignace to pick up Father Marquette. On May 17, 1673, Father Marquette, Jolliet, and five other men left Saint Ignace in two canoes made from the bark of birch trees. They sailed along the western shore of Lake Michigan toward the Fox River. Every day they traveled about 30 miles (48 km). In the evenings they slept on land. Sometimes the water was so shallow that the canoes would scrape along the river bottom. During these times, the men had to get out and carry the canoes until the water was deep enough to sail again.

Top: This photo shows the Fox River, where Marquette and Jolliet sailed in 1673. Middle: This map shows Marquette and Jolliet's route along the Mississippi River. Bottom: In this picture, the two explorers are shown sailing in canoes.

LAKE SUPERIOR

Sault
Ste. Marie

Saint Ignace

Wisconsin River

Mississippi River

Fox River

LAKE HURON

LAKE MICHIGAN

Portage
June 17, 1673

Illinois River

Missouri River

Illinois River

Ohio River

Arkansas River

Missouri River

July 17, 1673

Smoking in Peace

During the first few weeks, the expedition came across many friendly Native Americans. Both Father Marquette and Jolliet spoke several Native American languages. In early June, the Menominee tribe warned them about unfriendly Native Americans who lived along the river. On June 7, the Maskouten tribe welcomed the expedition. The Maskoutens lived along the shore of the Fox River, below Lake Winnebago. They asked Father Marquette and Jolliet to smoke a **calumet**, or a peace pipe. Father Marquette and Jolliet smoked the calumet with the Maskouten chiefs as a sign of peace. Two Maskouten men agreed to guide the expedition to the Wisconsin River. Marquette and Jolliet hoped that this river would lead them to the Mississippi.

Above: *This is a picture of a calumet, or peace pipe.* Top Left: *In this picture, Father Marquette is being offered a calumet by a Native American.* Bottom Left: *This photo shows what a missionary chapel in a Menominee lodge would have looked like.*

Into the Mississippi

After leading the expedition to the Wisconsin River, the Maskouten guides returned home. On June 17, 1673, Father Marquette and Jolliet reached a spot where the Wisconsin River turned into a much larger body of water. They had reached the Mississippi River. They saw huge fish that swam to the surface of the water and banged into the canoes. They also saw large herds of buffalo on the shores of the river. On June 25, the expedition saw human footprints in the mud along the riverbank. They decided to meet the people who lived there. They soon met members of the Illinois tribe, who welcomed the French explorers.

Above: This painting shows a herd of buffalo. Top Right: This is a painting of Marquette and Jolliet with their Native American guides. Bottom Right: In this painting, Marquette and Jolliet greet members of the Illinois tribe.

IN · HONOR · OF
LOUIS · JOLLIET · & · PÈRE · JACQUES · MARQUETTE

20

Dangerous Water

The Illinois tribe had warned Father Marquette and Jolliet of strange monsters that might attack them farther down the river. A few days later, the expedition saw rocks with monsters painted on them. The Frenchmen thought the paintings were a sign of warning. Past the rocks, the expedition reached the place where the Missouri River empties into the Mississippi. It was a dangerous place for canoes because the two rivers crashed together, creating **whirlpools** and **rapids**. Many days later, they passed the place where the Ohio River empties into the Mississippi. In early July, the expedition saw Native Americans shouting while waving bows, arrows, and hatchets in the air. Father Marquette stood up in the canoe to motion to the Native Americans. He took the calumet that the Illinois tribe had given him and held it in the air. The Native Americans recognized this sign of peace and invited the expedition to come ashore.

 Top: *In this picture, Father Marquette holds up a calumet as a sign of peace to a Native American tribe.* Bottom: *This sign honoring Marquette and Jolliet is hung over the Chicago River in Chicago, Illinois.*

21

Returning Home

On July 17, 1673, Father Marquette and Jolliet decided to return home. As the expedition traveled upstream, Jolliet checked the maps he had drawn during the long journey. Father Marquette and Jolliet both kept journals that recorded all they had seen. Father Marquette became sick on the journey home. He decided to stay at a mission near the Fox River. On May 17, 1675, Father Marquette died. Jolliet returned to Quebec, where he died in 1700. These two explorers always will be remembered, however. Their amazing journey along the Mississippi led the way for further explorations in North America.

Marquette and Jolliet's Timeline

1637   Jacques Marquette is born in Laon, France.

1645   Louis Jolliet is born in a settlement near Quebec, New France.

1673   On June 17, Marquette and Jolliet's expedition reaches the place where the Wisconsin River empties into the Mississippi.

1675   Father Marquette dies.

1700   Louis Jolliet dies.

Glossary

calumet (KAL-yuh-met) A peace pipe.

convert (kun-VERT) To change religious beliefs.

expeditions (ek-spuh-DIH-shunz) Trips for special purposes, such as a scientific study.

geography (jee-AH-gruh-fee) The study of Earth's surface, climate, continents, countries, and people.

harpsichord (HARP-sih-kord) An instrument similar to a piano, with two keyboards.

Jesuit (JEH-shyoo-wit) A member of a Roman Catholic religious order that is officially called the Society of Jesus.

lieutenant governor (loo-TEH-nent GUH-vuh-nur) An official who ranks one step below a governor, and serves as the governor's second in command.

merchant (MUR-chint) A person whose business is buying goods and selling them for profit.

missions (MIH-shunz) Religious centers that help people in a community.

missionaries (MIH-shuh-ner-eez) People who teach their religion to people with different beliefs.

ordained (or-DAYND) When someone is formally given a religious position, such as a priest or rabbi.

settlement (SEH-tul-ment) A small village or group of houses.

rapids (RA-pidz) The parts of a river where water flows very fast.

whirlpools (WURL-poolz) Currents of water that move quickly in a circle.

Index

C
calumet, 17, 21
Canada, 6
canoes, 14, 18
China, 13
Christians, 6

I
Illinois tribe, 18, 21

J
Jesuit, 5, 10
Jolliet brothers, 11

L
Laon, France, 5

M
Maskouten (tribe), 17, 18
Menominee tribe, 17
missionary, 5, 13
Mississippi (River), 17, 18, 21, 22
Missouri River, 21

N
Native Americans, 6, 9, 13, 17, 21
New France, 6, 10, 13

P
priest(s), 5, 6, 10

Q
Quebec, 9, 22

R
Reims, France, 5

S
Saint Ignace, 6, 13, 14
Sault Sainte Marie, 6, 11, 14

T
Talon, Jean Baptiste, 11, 13
Three Rivers, 6, 10

W
water route, 13
Wisconsin River, 17, 18

Web Sites

To learn more about Jacques Marquette and Louis Jolliet, check out these Web sites:

www.vmnf.civilization.ca/explor/explcd_e.html

www.win.tue.nl/~engels/discovery/jolmar.html